Plants in My World

PICKING FRUIT

Mark Ripley

PowerKiDS
press

NEW YORK

Published in 2018 by The Rosen Publishing Group, Inc.
29 East 21st Street, New York, NY 10010

First Edition

Editor: Theresa Morlock
Book Design: Michael Flynn

Photo Credits: Cover JMichl/Getty Images; p. 5 Arthur Linnik/Shutterstock.com; p. 6 images72/Shutterstock.com; p. 9 Daxiao Productions/Shutterstock.com; p. 10 Hanna Chernukha/Shutterstock.com; p. 13 martiapunts/Shutterstock.com; p. 13 (inset) MK photograp55; p. 14 alexpro9500/Shutterstock.com; p. 17 Larisa Blinova/Shutterstock.com; p. 18 Oksana Trautwein/Shutterstock.com; p. 21 Richard Speck/Gety Images; p. 22 ericmichaud/Getty Images.

Cataloging-in-Publication Data

Names: Ripley, Mark.
Title: Picking fruit / Mark Ripley.
Description: New York : PowerKids Press, 2018. | Series: Plants in my world | Includes index.
Identifiers: ISBN 9781508161639 (pbk.) | ISBN 9781508161653 (library bound) | ISBN 9781508161646 (6 pack)
Subjects: LCSH: Fruit–Juvenile literature.
Classification: LCC SB357.2 R57 2018 | DDC 634–dc23

Manufactured in China

CPSIA Compliance Information: Batch #BS17PK: For Further Information contact Rosen Publishing, New York, New York at 1-800-237-9932

Please visit: www.rosenpublishing.com and www.habausa.com

CONTENTS

Tasty Fruits

Apples and cherries are red, tasty fruits that grow on trees. Fruit trees grow on farms called orchards.

At the Orchard

Farmers take care of orchards. Farmers plant trees, water them, and keep them healthy. When fruit is ripe, farmers pick it. This is called harvesting.

There are thousands of different kinds of apples. Honeycrisp apples are crunchy and sweet. Granny Smith apples are green and tart. What's your favorite kind of apple?

Apple trees grow blossoms in the spring. Blossoms are the flowers that grow on trees. Most kinds of apple trees don't grow fruit until they are five years old.

Cherries

Unlike apples, cherries are stone fruits. Stone fruits are fruits that have hard pits, which hold the plant's seeds. Peaches and avocados are stone fruits, too.

All cherries can be put into two groups.

Sour cherries are the cherries used in pies.

Sweet cherries are often eaten fresh.

Sweet cherries are larger than sour cherries. Sweet cherries can be yellow, red, or dark purple. Sour cherries are small and dark red in color.

Picking Fruit

Cherries are good for you! Did you know that eating cherries can help you if you have a headache? Eating cherries can even help you sleep more soundly!

Cherry trees usually grow fruit when they're four years old. Thousands of cherries can grow on just one tree. Make sure you take the pits out of cherries before you eat them!

21

Picking fruit can be so much fun!

Ask your family if you can visit an orchard.

You can choose your very own delicious apples and cherries.

WORDS TO KNOW

avocado

blossom

pit

INDEX